RoguePoetry Review

2015

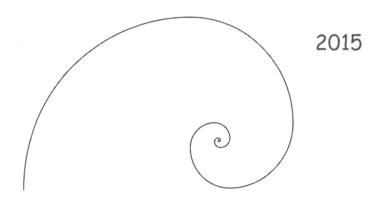

RoguePoetry Review

Catalog#: PWP002

Individual works: rights belong to their specified author

ISBN-10: 0986170712
ISBN-13: 978-0-9861707-1-3

www.punkswritepoems.com

Note from the Editor:

The first person I ever considered a fan was my Mother. This book would not exist without her. Unfortunately, she will never hold this in her hands. She will never read the words of the poets contained herein.

RoguePoetry Review is dedicated to the loving memory of:

Patricia Ann Bates

We held a contest on Tumblr, #wildcardwritingprompt. We asked our followers to write a poem with the prompt "the sky falls every night" and they delivered! You will find five poems (*) in this book from that contest.

Note from the Artist:

Margaret M. Bauman lives and works in the foothills of the Blue Ridge Mountains in Loudoun County, Virginia. She graduated with a BFA from Carnegie Mellon University with a dual focus in Painting and FiberArts. The work on the cover represents her fiber work which incorporates paper price tags manipulated and assembled into thematic wall art. The series, based on the Fibonacci sequence, was the focus of her most recent gallery exhibition from which these detail images were taken.

Margaret was very pleased and honored to be asked to provide artwork for the issue dedicated to her sister Patricia Bates and the images represented in the mono-print (page 45) are pulled from childhood memories...Patti's blue cat eye glasses, her cut-off Beethoven sweatshirt, "Follow Me' her solo as Nimueh, The Lady of the Lake in a production of Camelot to name a few.

Contents

Contents (cont.)

Shakespeare's Women

Hamlet's madness held her
Head down
While she was
Off picking flowers,
He wasn't there,
He'd pawned her already,
He was shooting arrows
And playing pirate,
While the sky fell for
Her every night,
But it was his choice
And his wet hands
Nonetheless.

Othello's blackness
Was so much nobler
Than the whiteness
Which "forced" his hands
To take her breath away
With a pillow. But it was
A man's choice,
A man's hands,
That made the sky
Fall every night,
And it was his man's hands
Who made her blame herself
Nonetheless.

Tamora's boys
Laid hands on his daughter,
Took her, her hands, her voice
And her choice; and
Titus lost his mind,
His hand, his sons,
His own sky had fallen
From his fatherly choices,

So, he chose to take her
Life for his honour with the
Hand that ought heal her
Nonetheless.

Real tragedy is
Every nightfall
Celebrating tragic heroes,
But not the tragedy
That falls every night
From their
               Hands
Nonetheless.

on this rain-soaked day

amidst wayward wind
watching the highway no. 33, through the moving window
the distant hills
and miles and miles
of swaying grass - a train cutting through
all these, whistling; homebound

I forgive
myself. . .

at the KFC

three tables down there
a lonely gypsylike girl watching
something in her cellphone
intently. . .

her coffee
my coffee

both getting cold. . .

it's a nice sunny day and suddenly we see the border--

the concrete six feet pillar says 'India No. 302'

we move on
towards Nepal, hear phone poles hum
see a cow and a calf
afraid, silently watching our SUV move away

almost two --
there's a brick kiln somewhere over there
vickey, the driver winks at me
says he's hungry and we stop at a roadside dhaba

order some tandoori chicken and a bottle
of whiskey

a few meters away
at the junction
of NH 07 and SH 44

a few more trucks roll by
kicking up dust, dead flowers
level, dry. . .

Zan Bockes

At Stake

So much
is at stake
lest
we forget
the warm kitchen
filled with
light.

Torture Me for Falling Down

This morning I wake to a sun-soaked bed, my nameless body better off dead, my head filled with goo gluing my impudence and its innocence onto the yellow mountain where sun never sets--at least, not for long. I am forlorn with sweet memories, when I crawled crooked across a dirty floor, got splinters in my palms. I've posted a proposition on my home's sick walls: Trade love for hate. But wonder thunders its tuneless good-byes, its preference for slender thighs. I'm worn out from saving the demons who collect in my heart like toll booths on the highway of broken desires; I can't hold myself up, a rag doll in frenzied free-fall, the scent of descent sharp in my nose--the pain of impact tastes too hot as I toss between rot and better not, the bitter pleas on my tongue.

Linda Crate

a liar named death

solemn

we walked
as if we were in a death march
maybe we were
killing our souls to see how
many times we could
live,
and i remember reaching for your hand
only for you to reject it
as if it were
inappropriate to be anything less
than unhappy;
but i insisted upon being cheerful all the same
perhaps that's why you began to despise
me
and our love died like all the flowers
you gave me—
the lilies and the roses and daisies
don't remember me,
but i recollect
them;
wonder why you even put forth the effort for
such a sweet lie but then again there's always the
need to make a lie seem
accurate
even if it isn't a truth
no one would know that better than you.

Pour la Lune

If you are the sun,
I am the moon beside you--
Dimmer but shining.

Each of my exhales
Rises up to meet the moon
To whisper secrets

The full moon is proud
Outshining the biggest stars
Without any fire

Father and mother
Nourishing and guiding us
The sun and the moon

As the moon waxes
After our newest re-birth,
We strive to evolve.

Hal O'Leary

A Failed Man

A failed man, some say that I must be,
A man society cannot endure,
But could society have failed me,
With promise I rejected as a lure?

A man society cannot endure,
Is one who will not bow to their demands
With promise I rejected as a lure,
They told me son, that that's the way it stands.

Is one who will not bow to their demands
A threat to them, their social peace of mind?
They told me son, that that's the way it stands.
Suggesting, if I fail, I'm unrefined.

A threat to them, their social peace of mind,
Society would put me on a shelf,
Suggesting, if I fail, I'm unrefined,
A man who only wants to be himself.

Society would put me on a shelf,
But could society have failed me,
A man who only wants to be himself.
A failed man? Some say that I must be.

Not me.

(The pantoum originated in Malaysia in the fifteenth-century as a short
folk poem, typically made up of two rhyming couplets that were recited
or sung. However, as the pantoum spread, and Western writers altered
and adapted the form, the importance of rhyming and meter diminished
but I have chosen to retain them both which represents to me the
discipline all art must have. The modern pantoum is a poem of any
length, composed of four-line stanzas in which the second and fourth
lines of each stanza serve as the first and third lines of the next stanza.
The last line of a pantoum is often the same as the first. - Hal O'Leary)

Winston Plowes

gap effects

Disorder over condition?

menace turns a tribute of speed into crisis.
The essence of jaded seconds breached.

a gap in fresh Young doubts
might open in the waning afternoon.

A pledge can be too little in return
When the hapless are suspended in credit.

(All the above words were found in The Guardian match report by Kevin
McCarra where England drew 2-2 with Switzerland on Monday 6th June
2011 at Wembley Stadium. All original case and punctuation preserved.)

Leveller

He has ignored the tortured shuffling at night
The severe photograph close beside them

it was a disturbing reminder
of 28 years ago
and not to be trusted
yet this free-spiritedness
never slipped

In a final beautiful day
The Metalist resistance said
"be proud of what we did.
Risks have to be embraced"
rise up and relish the fight

(All the above words were found in The Guardian match report by Kevin
McCarra where Portugal beat Holland 2-1 at Euro 2012 on Sunday 17th
June at the Metalist Stadium, Kharkiv. All original case and punctuation
preserved.)

stalemate Hold

unsettle the repertoire

of this Old and lofty City's Hart.
        notable Robert

his intense deadlock,
dull-hunger.
cared little for
foundations of A lost night.
        circumspectly Alex

(All the above words were found in The Guardian match report by Kevin
McCarra of a match between Manchester City and Manchester United on
10th November 2010. September. All original case and punctuation
preserved.)

Justin Antioho

It's hard to live in a painting

Hours and hours peel away
pushing the sweat along the wood grains
trying to reveal something new,

low wage has become an art for some
the pressure is driven into the dead,

it's Christ like
in forms of resurrection
the lonely carpenters trying to live
underneath
it's grating surfaces,

who is this for
when it's all said & done
for bankers & litigators is my guess
towering over the streets
where the bread is baked
& the soup is lines,

but maybe it's art
living against the grains
building something up away from the must,

it can't be easy
but it's blessed in galleries.

Darkness Falls

Dawn
An intrusive caress
A cold hand
Waking, rousing, rising
I place the mask in place
Practice my smile in the mirror
When the sky wakes
I will be ready

The effort all but wasted
Busy street
No eyes meet
We're all busy here
No time
For genuine
Sincerity
No matter
As long as you've got the smile

High noon now
My plastic face is hurting
Endurance
Key to survival
It's the trivial that keeps us safe
Lunch meeting
Means we can avoid
Going too deep

Evening again
Second wind
Just a few more hours to go
I adjust the mask over dinner
Wine sips
Small talk

Even the ones who claim to love me
Can't see through

Isolation
By the light of the moon
I can breathe again
Gravity
Pulling me towards salvation
The darkness of my reprieve
The certainty of my faith

The sky falls every night

Grains of Sand

imagine

crossing the Sahara

with the Tuareg;

sleeping

under one vast canopy of stars,

consoled by constellations

that once looked down

on ancient forests

and wind worn mountains

older than these here now.

it all repeats itself-

the river beds and rocks

return to the sea,

where temporary strangers

sit like Robinson Crusoe

on loud, tractor raked beaches

in smells of salt and dog shit

watching the waves,

thinking inside them

coming and going

like friends to be afraid of-

as nature retunes herself

ignoring our significance

becoming grains of sand.

weeds left,

wilt in the sun

without work and water.

their seeds

are the wild flowers,

waiting for volcanic wind

and ash to fall,

so the fertile cinders

can colonise herbacious borders

ending the old age

of selfish sediment

treading it down

in molecules of time.

another marxist

dons his trenchcoat

and tears pages from his red book

planting the old words

of revolution

in minds of homogenous compost.

over-privileged gallows begin to swing.

bullets sweat in their chambers

waiting for the right heads.

Genocide Princess

My fingers danced through
her barbed wire hair and
came out covered in
crimson chemtrails
and stars. She
laughed and sang ransom
demands until we drifted
awake. I traced the
childhood nightmares painted
across her skinny
wrists onto my
every thought where they
will remain until
the world stops
crafting bombs. She told me
that she was so
sick of the sky falling
every morning. Now I
stand outside and catch
every
single
piece
between my teeth while
she dissolves in the arms of
another victim but
I still crack
a clouded smile because
everything I do, I do
in the name of
her depravity.

Larry Corey

More Voices

By the snapping of a twig,
you will hear them.

By the mouth of the grave,
they will be heard.

You will hear them
in the song of the peacock,
in the voice of the turtle,
in the kiss of a toad.

Speaking.

In the upper chamber,
in tongues of fire

speaking

to old men
and young boys
washing their feet.

Listening
And there will be
bread from the ground,
grapes from the vine,
and water from their hands.

And voices calling
from under the rock.

"*Come,*" they call,
"*come under the rock,
under the bread,
among the grapes
drowning in wine.*"

Single Use Only

I saw paper plates on a wedding registry list.
China is pretentious, the bride said, besides,
you can't put it in the dishwasher.

The corner diner used to serve on earthenware
but Juliet was also known as butterfingers
so the owner switched to acrylic—he said it bounces.

Paper has always been the choice for food kitchens.
Heavier soups will seep through, but it's easy to clean
and less likely to sprout legs.

On the morning after, I couldn't sleep in a strange bed.
Bored, I decided to make some coffee
and woke you while searching the cabinets.

You thanked me with a disposable smile
as you pulled a couple of styrofoam cups
from the shelf right next to the porcelain mugs.

Royal Cleanup in Aisle 12

My nose was in the butt end of a cantaloupe
when I saw the cardinal flash near the potatoes,
causing me to wonder if the local crop duster
had slipped some phencyclidine
into last week's aerial application.

Melons forgotten, I slipped past
the grape clusters, trying to not sniff
as I rounded the onions to find her
inspecting the Granny Smiths for bruises.

Mimicking red-fire lettuce,
taffeta billowed around her legs
while sequins tried to cover
her overly ripe honeydews.

Fluorescents caught in her tiara
as she waved across the Valencias;
elbow-elbow-wrist-wrist.

By way of her carrot scepter
she bestowed upon me damehood,
so I curtsied into the kumquats.

It was then that I noticed
her scuffed Payless heels
and shredded lace on her hem.

She offered an aristocratic smile
as her prickly pineapple palms
pushed her empty cart towards
the revolving door.

Cafe au Lait

I gave up Mr. Coffee for a French Press,

the single, since Nancy only drinks

Pepsi in the morning, it takes up less

space in our cramped apartment,

I can brew one cup, strong and dark

as I like, just for me, though today I wonder

will I be able to share it with Luc

or Pierre, or whatever his name is,

the backpacker from Biarritz who is in

my bed, his rucksack on the floor,

his best friend from university

in the bed down the hall with Nancy and her

magnificent breasts, she always gets

the cuter ones, thanks for the mammaries,

Luc or Pierre having a crooked nose

or a chipped tooth but it doesn't matter,

I've heard the perfect faces are selfish

lovers, who urge - as Whitman said -

urge and urge and urge, always

the procreant urge of the world - only

it's the greedy urge of the dick for Nancy,

what is French for dick, do they co-opt our slang

and say dicque, and Pierre, I'll stick with Pierre,

with his cubist face like Picasso painted him,

yes Pierre, his tongue and fingers like

paintbrushes outlining me until

I cry out, I'm a work of art now, springing

from the canvas of sheets tangled around

him, panting, breathing life into my gasp,

Do you even have French presses in Paris,

or are they like French fries, and my

lopside-faced lover looks puzzled and sleepy

so I say, never mind, you can have

the whole cup.

Love on a Bus

I took Greyhound from Key West to California.

2,600 miles and nothing

but love/hate in New Orleans near the transfer station.

We already knew each other on that broken bathroom sink.

Pink neon light flash through the window.

Blink-thrust. Blink-thrust.

Wasn't like fresh love *chooga chooga* in a sleeping car outside Chicago.

Train whistle anonymity.

Two strangers fall in the top bunk and live happily ever Cary Grant-like.

Never happens that way on a bus.

Kelly Neal

where what's unfolded

at a juncture

an opening

a newer door

Where stands now

lost within motion's quandary

indecisive as ever

so hobbled by possibility's

endless expansion

and narrow causality's

strict flower

hesitant

he enters

again and again

in pursuit of one

moment which stays

still here

framed in eternity

Older Woman Seeks Companionable Mate

tall, thin, drives an old Ford truck
wears a cowboy hat, never a baseball cap
loves dogs, Pink Floyd, Puccini
bacon, prairies, wears a necklace
of chunky stone, cowboy boots
straight tight jeans, pearl-snap
plaid shirt or white tie
holds his arm for me but doesn't
always open doors
rises at dawn, gets dirty
then cleans up good with a faint
expensive scent trailing him
like a faithful hound

sleeps on the ground or a feather
bed, builds a mean campfire
fishes a little, hikes or rides
knows stars, birds, flowers,
knots, computers, clouds
cooks omelets, biscuits, chili
not pies, drinks good beer,
no Coors Light, and dark
tea, likes cool blue sheets
strong arms in bed, light kisses
alone, keeps a neat bathroom,
sock drawer, workshop of oiled
tools, polishes his boots,

irons shirts, handles a broom—

no dusting— sews buttons

sews wounds

reads widely, tells the truth

knows who I really am—

an old woman, knows himself

too— unruffled, solid

implacable rock with soft

edges, an edgy stream

in cool desert sunrise,

a green forest noon.

Maybe an ad in the paper will do.

Locus

We talk through the thick blackened sun;

this is foolish. Your life is elsewhere.

And when I live my life, here, you

often fail to cross my mind. Then, like

a sudden fog horn, your ship comes

to shore; you are not aboard. I make love

to the captain, who could be Adam

and the first sin. I would rather a woman,

her back rigid with muscle, staring

out to sea, where I drift. Such concern.

She knows how to forgive inclement weather,

at the break of the sun from the sky

when color collapses forsaken into night.

Karin Krötlinger

Excursion

We walked gingerly, our spines perpendicular
with effort to keep our distances from overlapping;

In a room of blackwood cushioned with a century
of marvel, frog-fish and anemones swept the surface

of the vitrines, eyes full of afterlife; I stopped to stare
at a sea-devil when your elbow brushed the tattoo

someone who piously suicided in an abbey's campanile
designed for my protection; You pointed toward

the marsupials and I snuck my hand in yours to skip
long drinks for the tacit lack of a sequel.

A. Lebron

Four Truths

Our memories are stains;
I've worked fervently to cut out.

Bleach couldn't lift you;
I prepared a sacrifice.

I'd rather destroy a part of me
than continue carrying you around.

I've taught myself to live
with holes in my heart.

World in Review

When did people
stop being people?
How did humanity
become structured labels;
A room full of assigned seats?

Brian Rowe

Hands

Age spots, freckles, and veins disappear

In the tropical wonderland.

Flipping them from side to side

Makes stallions blink to admire

The ten long pointy toothpicks.

Bracelet marks open the gate to

An island of longevity.

I need to know if there is any way

To find a state of peace

In the waves slowly seeping onto the beach.

Don't feel obligated, you say,

There's always fishing in the Pacific.

I'm a Riot

A fit of laughter

A fist in the air

Lungs burning

From the inability to inhale

Raucous merriment

Outcry against pessimism

That tries to infect

But laughter...

A smile, a small joy

Are far more infectious

If you let it take hold

Of your mouth

Of your heart

Riot with me

Aaron B. Jackson

Dying Parent

What would Ginsberg think?

Of me

Standing next to his organ

In a museum for

Beats

Cell phone ringing

Mom calling

From across the country

Dad

Is back in the

Hospital

His stomach has broken

A routine part

Of

His

Cancer

At this point

No punctuation other than apostrophes

Fucking fuck it I can't concentrate
I am unable to concentrate seeing as can't is not a word
Cannot you may get away with
I feel so shy of any inspiration
I feel so epileptic
And yet still have a lot to do to be productive
I'm out of pills and my headache is growing
I've a knot in my hair that I am pulling

Bottle teats rubber
Ducks
Quack docs
To type on making messy
Fingerprinting all over that clean white page

People don't reply to my texts and it annoys me
especially if it's a conversation we're having
and it's about a problem I need help in resolving

This computer is so shaky
Quaking as my belly rumbles against its wooden top throne
it is seated upon

I have no patience for stories nor for libraries that close early

John Saunders

Thinking of Sophie Sondheim

Freshly picked cherries
the colours of red and black-
soft wet-shiny skin,
sweet on my lips.
Collioure is an imagination of colour
in the summer light.

She is somewhere around here,
probably drinking cold beer
with the boys,
her artist's model face
a pale ochre,
her hair a tangle of draped curl.

How we might share these fruits
of languorous kisses,
taste the earth on our tongues.
This is bliss and tragedy.
The white yachts sail out to sea,
wash my dreams away.

In/On

firm foundations don't always birth grand buildings
fantasize

- garage, lo-fi aspirations

.

and, statues. dolls. action figures.

models.

-

where rage is the raisin gentle light – the grape

expression – wine

.

tableaux silent

as

rain splashes pasture

.

coworkers exit and never return

faith is set in stone plans are carved in sand washed away as
soon as agreed upon

remember, let's try strife and stick where feet sto(m)p.

travelling is not the same as wandering. silence enjoyed
sleeping in the morning's
brew

all that's wanted/needed = a seat, a place meant for

aches to heal. for words to abuse meaning. where there is

chasing and floating. remained impacted. intact, living in

a world beyond townships sailing into sets assembled and painted
by . . .

David Antonio Moody

from *What Wish Under Your Pillow Isn't Teeth*

But silly me: leather

and the ankle heel.

Boots
in the old way and boots
for fucking up

shit in the mosh pit of an afterlife
crowd. What Jesus
rocks hair.

What many hands
of Hindu gods finger
strings ever amped.

Ever is the ghost
of a memory walking
of harm and how
once the haunter was made

out of bugs, for lo,
was not the hornet
in the hot tub fugazi

waiting
for a wet man
to touch
and be touched?

And who says what wish
under your pillow isn't
teeth, a coin, a pistol, flowers

or a way
to bite back,
grinning as a white rose does?

I am your yes man, you said. *I meant* wet.
I am your yes man, but be your own pet.

for tomorrow we do it all over again

the sky falls every night

we catch it in
martini glasses, tumblers,
mason jars
   it is oily, thick
we stir it with swizzle sticks
and watch it swirl, purple-dark,
blue-black, picking up a glint
of copper when it reflects
the moon
   which perches, a golden
garnish, on the sugared rims

"a toast," we say,
and drink
   until we're hollowed out,
   until we're full
of the tart sweet taste
   of the evening's sad love

when the glasses have been drained
we set them aside and watch
as the stars crack
and melt like ice cubes,
   one by one,

   and disappear

David Seaman

Determination's Ideation

Passion's backdoor swings open again tonight.

The cold wind causes it to creak loudly.

A lantern casts an eerie glimmering

light rocking in time to my beating heart.

My home of safety is this disturbed tonight

by voices whispered on the wind.

Dark allure has come for me again,

inviting the dreadful to taunt my rest,

titillating that dark softness of heart.

Oh let them fucking take me now!

My spirit is sick from the fighting devil.

To what end would I prevail against him

when my mind is yet to be concluded.

"Let us journey then!" I shout.

The river yowls on the night wind

from the woodland behind passion's hill side.

Such a wretched blunder to heed the demon.

Lost forever in my still broken black heart.

Black Coffee

Do I want room for cream?

No. I order my coffee black,
"black as death,"

which isn't funny,
especially when the three washed-out punks
to my left start chanting:

"I love coffee. I love espresso. I love death..."
which sounds familiar, but instead
of realizing that they're mocking me,

I assume they're quoting Black Flag,
or maybe Nietzsche, and it's true
that they're slamming double espressos

with a jittery, loose-bolt gusto.
They're quoting the black holes in their mugs.
They're quoting a pack of wolves.

They're quoting the half-naked beggar
who asks for immortality
but accepts a handful of change.

They are mocking life's oddness
and darkness and clever old farts
who only find solace in the words of tin gods.

Laura Taylor

Jigsaw

stealing pieces of experience
to place them just outside of your own

j

    i

           g

    s

    a

    w

    y   our

semiotic symptom
of a need to reproduce;
connote two-tone heartbreak
tragedy ripped
from a 2D playground

second-hand realities
suck on ragged fragments
forcing them to f
          it

    every corner of the composite
                        un
clean

dirty littered grief-strewn jackdawed glory

no full balloon floats
under water
any more
than an empty swing
is saddled with distress.

Televisions of Our Future

You left so I leave
the television on to not feel
so alone.
Those that were strangers then
with voices now familiar
talk of things stranger than
just a ball being thrown.
You never took me up on that.

Hard to be the new man of the house
when mother won't stop pushing
her cheeks into a smile while
sisters twists wrinkles in her blouse.

To fill your large and weathered leather boots.

I found reassurance in watching what you did
when you got home from work.
But you never let me what the show you did –
too violent or I'm too young or no.

The couch still holds the silhouette you left
the television on.
I'll watch and learn because what
else is going to show me how to
be a man.

You always used to say that.

I looked for God outside of church,
those four walls always made you feel
trapped.

My knees became hard and red
like your knuckles.

A boy from school was mean to sister so
I made his body bleed on to the cement.
The blood from his nose pooled around him
like a shadow. Blood kept pouring out of him –
it looked like the horizon.

I saw myself no longer as your son.

You'd be proud,
my knuckles are hard and red.

Who needs a boyfriend when you have a record collection?

She's an ageless wonder with teenage lust,

selecting lovers like choosing vinyl's

from her eclectic LP collection

I long to be Jesus to her Mary Chain.

Her wrinkles are like song grooves

on record, while inhaling

her reddest flares, one touch fingers

that run through her endless hair

like chords that will have you

pleasing her Lord, will keep you spinning

speaking through her tongues

like some candy talking. Her lips are sweetest

when she laughs like Hope Sandoval

shaking hips, her body craving feedback

her riffing eyelids fading into you,

just like honey dripping Mazzy Stars.

I want to dip my microphone voice

in her timeless fountain and swim

in the ripples of her roller-coaster skies.

One night with her is like putting

the needle down on her favorite

turn-tabled spot, just a taste of her

own way of praying, one lick

of her guitar neck, smooth

addictive feedbacks her eternal

inner rhythms, speakers blown, stoned

and dethroned, leaving you naked,

returning the kind of 33 1/3 rpm

while shimmering reverberations

the deepest smiles; nails on skin

like pointed needles; this crackling

45 rpm single waxes erotically,

spinning hard enough to make you drop

Untethered

unfold your ribbons
those bands of milky way
have spread the comforter
as the sky falls
every night
so I can
know
what it's like
to float
over the moon

Allison Grayhurst

At the door

strenuous circulation, eclipsing slow knocking
for a faster ring - two times, ten times - no number
is sufficient to enlist satisfaction.
I am fatigued but not maturing, still devolved,
using sluggish generalizations with ingrained attitudes of defeat -
owner of tedium and isolation.
I circle the entrance, attempting to widen what
I trace but there is no way in, no probing
magnificent enough to fracture the tight curve,
and my spirit is different than it was when incense
eased my fixations. Chapter books
are passed over. Details do not help nor
do the angels when they sit beside me as they are now -
their hands over my neck and waist, and their low voices
humming to keep me swallowing, to keep me
from being swallowed: Nothing has changed
since I was 16 and left my home
and I circle - my tongue
a witness to the locks upon the gate. Index finger, thumb – their
dexterity and desire circling, wanting sensual ownership, malleable
distances narrowed and overridden, wanting to be
crazed with fullness, to turn the lamp on and read,
not have impatience rack across my flesh like it is
like surgical lasers and flashing letters I do not need. Because I need
a way in - to clean my house of this disordered ignorance,
to dive across the equator, burying myself in the heated air -
become an instrument of refraction, drilling into
unheard syllables, taste what's inside this closed-off cavity
and be received.

A Post War History of the Coffee Table

a middle class hero is something to be
composting the grounds of fair trade coffee
served in a mug made by amazonians
placed on a hand woven coaster sent
with love from far flung deepest africa

useful to stop rings on the table made
from resourced timber that came in flatpacks
ikea to home on a bicycle
and used almost ceremoniously
when guests come round for organic tea
and victoria sponge on recycled paper doilies

multi functional desk for the laptop
mum dad two point four perfect family
super fast broadband setting up online direct
debits for amnesty greenpeace adopt
an indian elephant and later

when dad's all alone with the curtains drawn
parental filters click history gone
the silent majority are quietly sticking
their fingers and vibrators up their holy arses for
the middle classes are a bunch of wankers
constantly wearing painted smugness even
when faking their contorted come faces

Paul Lamar

To the Young Man (for George)

I am the museum guard, so
of what use is a visitor to me?
I am on the lookout
for your thoughtless hands.

You don't know the floor
you're on. You can't wait
to eat when food is all
around you. You sit because
you're tired. You drift
and drift, a penny purchase
in your hand. Your map
is upside down. You stand
too close to see
"How it was done."

You pose. You tap. You sigh.
You shake your empty head
in mock appreciation.
You worry that you'll get
a parking ticket. Life
still sprawls before you.

Every night I get down
on the floor. What trips
I've taken! How many seas
I've sailed and bridges crossed,
and talks with queens
and fishermen. How many yards
and meadows walked,
how many curtains gazed behind.
How many battles fought!
How many dogs and lions stroked,
how many horses ridden.
When you become the guard,
I'll be paint or Degas' metal girl.

Seventh Shard

I.
I believe pedestrians lead me to closed
havens, or work, depending on the day,
and splinter my quiet-weekend bones.

II.
Last night, on an off-ramp impeded
by the I-71 crossover, we chipped paint
as we swerved too close to a raccoon
scrounging for plastic bottles. Too close,
each we think, when we're bound for cities
larger than ring-eyed Columbus.

III.
Someone yelled stop into the gray salt
morning Sunday. I stood and wouldn't
move. At the open market an Episcopalian
priest gave his twisted violet shawl
to a lady with a pink pleated sweater.

IV.
I picked fresh arugula at the open
market. I picked stripped beets
at the open market. I picked three apples
and a carrot at the open market
one rainy after-work walk.

V.
There were sticks in the road that
I wanted to throw at the man leering
at the car window to comb his hair.

VI.
He picked at the jar in boredom
and knew he would break the lid
the harder he pressed. It turns me on
when metal uplifts the glass ridge,
a quick pop and silence in his hand.

VII.
At Green Sands, I heard a turtle bubble
on the rocks. If you turn a faucet
slow enough, you can hear it, too.

Paul Hostovsky

Poem Beginning with a Last Line from Dubliners

In my heart I had always despised him a little.
He was very well read, hopelessly intelligent,
soulless. For example, he would probably
recognize the line, and the story it's borrowed from--
'stolen' from, he would say--but he wouldn't get
the poem. Which is why I feel compelled to write it.
We were both English majors at an obscure little
liberal arts college that catered to creative fuck-ups
on the Hudson. I'd read a little Joyce in high school.
He said he'd read *all* of Joyce, including *Finnegan's Wake*
twice, and a biography of Nora Barnacle, which
"helps explain Joyce's scatological bent," he said.
His girlfriend and my girlfriend shared the same first name,
only spelled differently. He said he'd done *everything*
with her, including some things he said I couldn't imagine.
I said I was pretty sure I'd already imagined everything
one could do with a girl. That's when he gave me
his shit-eating grin, lit his pipe which had gone out
in the meantime, sucked on it vigorously until
a cloud of brownish smoke subsumed his head and most of
the upper half of his body. "Not this, you haven't,"
he said. Then he told me things that both disgusted
and aroused me. They disgusted me first, then aroused
me later after going over and over them in a kind of
holding pattern in my head. I wavered about whether
to tell my girlfriend, judging not to in the end. Thus
she remained innocent of it, as though I'd changed
her name, to protect her, the way they do in novels.
Her name was Melodie, spelled that way and not the other.

The Big Heat

It has to be the heat.
No human hands could
tease hair that high.
And temperature shortened
the skirt,
undid the buttons,
and the heels...
surely melted down
until just the stiletto remained.

Humidity, the usual refrain.
Must count for the way she walks,
the smothering liquid in the air
coaxing her rear end one way
while her head faces in another.
And would have wetted the lips
of the guys on the construction site too
but who whistles anymore.
The clamminess is red meat
to the beast.
Such names they hurl down
from the girders,
amplified if not encouraged
by the mugginess.

No way to cool down
on such a summer's day.
The sexiness just takes it.
The hormones sizzle
on the scaffolding
No winter of the girl
in flannel pajamas,
the boy in bed
reading his pirate book.
A hundred in the shade,
the news said.
And a hundred more
where that came from.

Vanishing Act

Somewhere someone disappears,
is discovered years later
loading the "It's A Small World" boats

at Disneyland
or singing in a gay men's chorus
on a tour of Japan -

so don't give up all hope -
it's a small world after all -
even gay, if you source the singing.

Golden Cup

At Golden Cup the money flies
Atop the stage to catch the eyes
Of solo girl engaged to dance
In hopes of buying him a chance
With her, alone, in only pasties.

The posted signs are all implied
Warnings: *No Fingers Past Thighs,*
Thanks For Your Patronage and Compliance
At Golden Cup.

For certain types of Janes and Johnnies
Dressed in designer links and ties
They offer off menu services
Without balk or consequence
Just expense for up front lies
At Golden Cup.

Stalling Winter's Morning
after James Wright

Ten more miles, it is Leon Iowa.
There the roads turn white,
When no one walks down them.
One more night of driving and I could have become
A whippoorwill, haunting
Dark's still sky, alone.

I have got this far. It is sunrise soon. But never mind time:
It is not alive.
It is still Missouri.
Among the frozen cornstalks, the light ripple
Of wind flutters to its death.
At least, it is silent again,
Although, between me and the empty silos
Snow falls like spent fire —
crumbling under touch.

The sun begins to spill. I hear the nightjar
Acquit herself,
She has flown out of the dark places behind me.
Ethereal and light she steals from my eyes
Each word I would to write.
She has lived a long time, she loves to riddle
No one knows her.

Yesterday I paced in City's buildings
And slept with his people, alone.
I come all this way, to surrender my song
To the call of a bird.

The Failures of Time Travel

Yellow in my eyes.

The yellow of egg yolks,

of traffic lights,

the color of voided potential.

I scroll backward through years,

to pin the moment where it all

turned rancid to the wall,

but it is not a moment.

It is a scattering of glass shards

across a gravel floor.

City

The city reminds me of you.

Streets as twisting as your voice,

narrow, sleek, echoing into my thoughts.

The hum of the city is

as warm as your hands

as it opens and closes in waves around me.

And the light.

Sun sharpening itself against glass,

bringing too much of you to life.

Nuke the Nazis

A man with a swastika for a hand asked me for a cigarette.
I gave one up, and lit it for him because the other was a
Spider bite, pockmarked with little teeth and oozing beneath
a bandage that held the SS emblazoned on his knuckles.
He could no longer move his fingers.

In his right hand, justice for the White cosmos,
In his left hand, in his ashy face, in his yellow
Jumpsuit pants, in his heart grown placid in mourning,
Shirt torn either from trying to claw it out
Or his heart escaping a new identity when the body,
Weary of slamming itself against a wall that only welcomed it back
With a breathing warm embrace, decidedly went gentle.

I looked at his face again, real close that time because second
glances
Are analytical and arguably matter more than the first
And saw the grave mark where Misjudgment, retributive
Archangel,
Most cruel in its divine wisdom of the seraphim,
Champion Too Little Too Late smote him from up high
In the circles where he once reigned King of Homogeneity,

Down to the icy streets
Where spiders hungrily gnawed the space around the SS on his
knuckles,
Maybe as a reminder of the timeless conflagrate kiss of an inward
death
That happened slowly after he condemned the World, realizing that
Indeed the white man will be its undertaker.

Down to miles and miles of trash and concrete which is really trash
too,
Where a cigarette from a stranger feels like redemption from the
world
        he pushed back against for so long.
Where the first drag feels like "welcome home" and the second
feels like "I'm here to stay," back underneath the same world's
skin.
I didn't forgive him for deciding to tote the banner of the Third
Reich, not that the act was mine to forgive as a white man,
Or that he even sought forgiveness at all.
But the spiders got him first.

The snow falling all around, the sorry guy metamorphosed into the
shopping center ghost, who's probably been bumming around here
in the ancient times before corporate gentrification—
I couldn't condemn him when he winced.
Deciding he had suffered enough,
Or maybe because I was scared,
I gave him a cigarette and lit it.
Either way, he looked humbled.

my psyche is not a Levittown schematic

with whimpering eyes I plead-
why hasn't he left?
doesn't he see?
or does he see and it doesn't matter?

what stone cairns have I built
to allow me to see out but no one in?

I'm so timeless
that at 43 I'm paying someone
to tell me to Let Go
when I could have paid
for good bread and watched Frozen

the strongest image I hold
from today
is how he put his arm around me
in the kitchen
without question when I reached for him
and with his other hand
helped our child with homework
-there's comfort there
that should be enough

she told me yesterday
I can be retrained
if I could unlearn the primal lessons
that I hold closest
wounding myself like an idiot
(maybe I paraphrased)

can't parlay with a dead man
but I'd love to ask
"what did you want from me, before you left?"

outsmarted by myself
no wonder I haven't caught a break
there's no schematic for what ails me
petulance in a fairy tale

today is a breaking sky

there are days that crack
like a moonbeam through a thicket
and then there are days that break
so wide it's as if the sun will burn all.

today is a breaking sky
with cymbals and waves and light.
perhaps it's hormones or chemicals-
I will not argue the results.

waking hips aching...
birth of new ideas...

icicles that taste of hope or spring
are just winter preserved as it should be,
and when we peel off gloves
to catch snow
it melts but first is very beautiful falling.

thoughts could roam free
across prairies and party lines,
but someone's there to hold the reins
unless we race the very sun
and make it ahead of shadows.

hungry loons

so close to that other side
please don't go
and leave me here

dampness only works
when we share heat
and banter

a taste of you
has only made me
more hungry

there's so much
I forgot

I know I'm not a dayglo kitten

itchy to strip away
all I can reach
I'd be raw

dousing rage
doesn't work well
naked

but to feel unfiltered breezes
would be worth the burn

you're not an answering loon

cool ripples moved
across carefully designed
cesspools

you know how delicious
it feels to savor muck
with me

we're immeasurably right
touching skin and hair
and teeth

let's answer hunger by moonlight

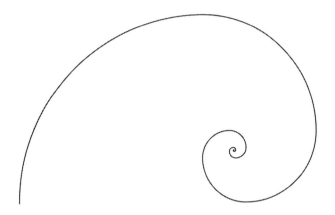

J.T. Antioho is a literature student and writer attempting to manage his existence in the southeastern Atlantic summers. He grew up on the cowville dividing line of Indiana and Michigan; beautifully marked, 'The RV Capital of the World.' What luck! He is unpublished, but works everyday to create something focusing on dreamscapes, art, philosophy, social issues, and history. When he's not trying to find words, time is mostly spent growing hot peppers, herbs and spices, and keeping his meagle Emerson from destroying it. For him, life is about collectivism, nature, the beard, and love.

Glen Armstrong holds an MFA in English from the University of Massachusetts, Amherst and teaches writing at Oakland University in Rochester, Michigan. He edits a poetry journal called *Cruel Garters* and has three new chapbooks: *Set List* (Bitchin Kitsch,) *In Stone* and *The Most Awkward Silence of All* (both Cruel Garters Press.) His work has appeared in *Conduit* and *The Puritan,* where they let him go on and on about Courtney Barnett as a guest blogger.

Hope Benefield is a retail sales associate in the suburban outlays of St. Louis, Missouri but enjoys writing poetry far more than answering the question: "where is the sour cream?" She has begun to suspect that the answer to this question is actually, perhaps, one of a deeper metaphysical nature. You may find more of her life and work at hopebe.tumblr.com.

Zan Bockes is a direct descendant of Bacchus, the Roman god of wine and revelry. She earned an MFA in Creative Writing from the University of Montana. Her fiction, nonfiction and poetry have appeared in many magazines and anthologies, including *Writers and Their Notebooks, Kaleidoscope, Out of Our, Cutbank* and *Phantasmagoria*, and she has had four nominations for a Pushcart Prize. Her collection of poetry, *Caught in Passing*, is available from Turning Point Books (WordTech Communications). She lives with her husband in a funky old house in Missoula, Montana, and supports her writing habit as a Residential Sanitation Specialist for her own housecleaning business.

Valentina Cano is a student of classical singing who spends whatever free time she has either reading or writing. Her works have appeared in numerous publications and her poetry has been nominated for the Pushcart Prize and Best of the Web. Her debut novel, The Rose Master, was published in 2014 and was called a "strong and satisfying effort" by Publishers Weekly.

Adrian Ernesto Cepeda is an L.A. poet whose work appears in the new *True Romance Poems* collection, *1000 Tankas for Michael Brown*, *The Lake Poetry*, *Edgar Allan Poet Journal # 2*, *Fukushima Poetry Anthology*, *The New Verse News*, *San Gabriel Valley Poetry Quarterly*, *Spilt Ink Poetry*, *Erotic T Magazine*, *Luna Luna Magazine's Latino Poetry Project*, *Love Poetry Lovers*, *Silver Birch Press*, *Transcendence Magazine*, *Ealain Literary & Art Magazine*, *ZO Magazine*, *Thick With Conviction*, *Oddball Magazine*, *The Rain, Party, & Disaster Society*, *Men's Heartbreak Anthology*, *Purrfect Poetry Anthology* and in the soon to be released Poetry in Motion's collection *Poems to Fuck to*. He is currently enrolled in the MFA Graduate program at Antioch University in Los Angeles

Kanchan Chatterjee is an executive, from Jamshedpur, Jharkhand India, working in the ministry of finance, government of India. Although he does not have any literary background, he loves poetry and scribbles as and when he feels the urge. His poems have appeared in various online and print journals, namely, 'Eclectic eel', 'Mad Swirl', 'Shot Glass Journal', 'Jellyfish Whisperer' , 'Bare Hands Poetry', 'River Muse', 'Decanto' 'Ygradsil' etc.

Pat Condliffe should be finishing a doctoral thesis at The University of Sydney, Australia; all too often Pat is abducted by creative urges that either end up on Tumblr, or corroding away in waste bins. When not procrastinating, Pat writes about hoax literature, horror, and westerns. In a former life Pat was a chef, and for a while a herder of goats in a Southern Spanish frontier town. Now he teaches and tries to corrupt innocent young minds with doctrines of fairness and equality. Pat lives in Sydney with his partner where they are raising two girls to be total badasses with a healthy appreciation for comic- books and the culinary arts. Pat's work has been published in *Southerly*, *The Rising Phoenix Review*, *Griffiths Review*, and *Media International Australia*. Pat was part of the editorial collective for *Philament, The University of Sydney Journal of the Arts*.

Larry Corey has published one poetry collection (THE KALIDAS VERSES) and a second (RATS' ALLEY POEMS) is on the way. His individual poems have appeared in literary magazines such as *Chaffey Review, Poetry Pacific, Empty Sink, Screech Owl, Snapping Twig, Pif, Evergreen Review, Beloit Poetry Journal, Zeek Choice,* and others. He lives with two pit bulls, one lab, and three cats in a small mountain community 7 thousand feet above sea level in the San Bernardino Mountains of SoCal.

Linda M. Crate is a Pennsylvanian native born in Pittsburgh yet raised in the rural town of Conneautville. Her poetry, short stories, articles, and reviews have been published in a myriad of magazines both online and in print. Recently her two chapbooks *A Mermaid Crashing Into Dawn* (Fowlpox Press - June 2013) and *Less Than A Man* (The Camel Saloon - January 2014) were published. Her fantasy novel *Blood & Magic* was published in March 2015.

Andira Dodge lives in rural Pennsylvania where she writes whenever she can and enjoys capturing the full range of seasons with her camera. She is the mother of two children and tries to outplay them as often as possible. After graduating from Temple University with a degree in journalism, she has worked for both a large corporate public relations firm and a small professional theater. She has had her work published, most often in independent online magazines. You may explore more of her work by visiting wordrummager.com.

The Arabella (more commonly known as **Brittany A. Estep**) is a strange creature. She appears rather normal at first glance. But if you watch closely enough and listen to the Arabella's incessant chattering you will find her to be quite intriguing. One of her defining characteristics is her creativity. She has enjoyed writing, crocheting, drawing and many other manner of artistic expression since she was a child. The Arabella is indigenous to the state of Georgia but in recent years migrated to South Carolina. She has a mate that she was joined to in ceremony several years ago. They have adopted animals outside their species to include two goofy dogs and a talkative cat. Her daily habits include stalking her preferred social media websites, working a part time job, college stuff, and scribbling and typing as much as possible. The staples of the Arabella's diet are strong cheeses and citrus.

Kenyatta Jean-Paul Garcia is the author of ROBOT, This Sentimental Education, Yawning on the Sands and Distilled and A Northern Elegy. Garcia was raised in Brooklyn, NY and currently resides in Albany, NY. Kenyatta has a degree Linguistics. In addition to writing, Kenyatta is the editor of ALTPOETICS and Sparks of Consciousness and is one half of the lo-fi noise punk pair - Hill Haints.

Allison Grayhurst is a member of the League of Canadian Poets. She has over 550 poems published in more than 275 international journals and anthologies. Her book *Somewhere Falling* was published by Beach Holme Publishers in 1995. Since then she has published eleven other books of poetry and six collections with Edge Unlimited Publishing. Prior to the publication *of Somewhere Falling* she had a poetry book published, *Common Dream*, and four chapbooks published by The Plowman. Her poetry chapbook *The River is Blind* was published by Ottawa publisher above/ground press in December 2012. More recently, her chapbook *Surrogate Dharma* was published by Kind of a Hurricane Press, Barometric Pressures Author Series in October 2014. She lives in Toronto with her family. She also sculpts, working with clay; www.allisongrayhurst.com

John Grey is Australian born poet, playwright, musician, short story writer, Providence RI resident since late seventies. . Has been published in numerous magazines from the scrappiest zines to the likes of Weird Tales, Christian Science Monitor, Greensboro Poetry Review, Poem, Agni, Poet Lore and Journal Of The American Medical Association as well as the horror anthology "What Fears Become" and the science fiction anthology "Futuredaze." Has had plays produced in Los Angeles and off-off Broadway in New York. Winner of Rhysling Award for short genre poetry in 1999.

Natasha Head is a Pushcart Prize nominated poet living and writing in Northern Ontario, Canada. She is the author of three collections of poetry and has had her work appear in numerous online and print publications, as well as the Academy of American Poets. She is a member of The League of Canadian Poets and part of The Winter Goose Publishing family. News and current daily poetry can be found at tashtoo.com

Paul Hostovsky is the author of seven books of poetry and six poetry chapbooks. His poems have won a Pushcart Prize and two Best of the Net awards. He has been featured on *Poetry Daily, Verse Daily,* and *The Writer's Almanac*. He makes his living in Boston as an interpreter for the Deaf. To read more of his work, visit him online at www.paulhostovsky.com

Aaron B. Jackson is a poet and writer. His poems have appeared in multiple publications including The Bark Magazine, Instigatorzine, Fat City Review and Runaway Parade, his work is also in many anthologies including Like One: Poems for Boston, Seeing Past Sickness, and works from Kattywompus Press and Cloud City Press. He is the former Poet Laureate of Jersey City, NJ (2005-06) and has twice been the recipient of grants from the Puffin Foundation. As a performer he has written and starred in a Partnership for a Drug Free America campaign and he also served as a poetry fellowship judge for the Connecticut Office of the Arts in 2013. Currently he is the Director of Visual Merchandising for the Strand Book Store. For more information please visit middlepoet.com.

Zane Johnson is a poet and musician from Denver, Colorado and is currently studying English at the Community College of Denver. His work has previously appeared in *The Rain, Party, and Disaster Society,* The Animal Liberation Front's *Activists+, Writing Raw,* and CCD's *Ourglass.* Most of his inspiration is drawn from his meditations and Buddhist practice, as well as the critical state of affairs of today's world. He defines his work as an honest inquiry into the nature and form of suffering today and the role of compassion in healing it. Zane also has plans to launch a print magazine in the Summer of 2015 dedicated to promoting compassionate social action in the United States. Updates on this, as well as more of his writing and meditations, can be found on quietresignation.tumblr.com.

Strider Marcus Jones — is a poet, law graduate and ex civil servant from Salford/Hinckley, England with proud Celtic roots in Ireland and Wales. A member of The Poetry Society, his five published books of poetry are modern, traditional, mythical, sometimes erotic, surreal and metaphysical http//www.lulu.com/spotlight/stridermarcusjones1. He is a maverick, moving between forests, mountains and cities, playing his saxophone and clarinet in warm solitude.
His poetry has been accepted for publication in 2015 by numerous publications, including And Agamemnon Dead (mgv2 Publishing Irish Poetry Anthology; Earl Of Plaid Literary Journal; Deep Water Literary Journal; Eccolinguistics; The Collapsed Lexicon Poetry Antho)logy; The Stray Branch Literary Magazine; Amomancies Poetry Magazine; East Coast Literary Review;Crack The Spine Literary Magazine; A New Ulster/Anu Issue 29/31; Outburst Poetry Magazine; The Galway Review; The Honest Ulsterman Magazine; Writing Raw Poetry Magazine;The Lonely Crowd Magazine; Section8Magazine; Danse Macabre Literary Magazine and The Lampeter Review.

Karin Krötlinger is a part time physiotherapist and full time insomniac. She also holds a tremendously useful degree in etching and writes in periods, taking the latter somewhat more seriously these days. She writes in German and English and currently bends spines into shape in Vienna/Austria.

Paul Lamar lives with his partner, Mark, in Albany, New York, where he teaches English part-time at a local college, writes theater reviews for a newspaper, and accompanies (piano) two choruses. They have three grown children and a delightful 10-year-old granddaughter, Hannah, who visits regularly.Over the years Paul has published poems in various magazines; as he zeroes in on 70 in September, gathering these pieces for a chapbook or two seems like the next logical step! Flash fiction has become a new passion. This bio sketch is being written on a three-week stay in Europe, where short-short story ideas keep coming at an alarming rate. Deo gratias.

A. Lebron is a freelance writer, an online blogger and a poet who was grown in New York City from Puerto Rican seeds. When she's not digging deep to write her truths and attend creative writing courses, she's usually stumbling through life trying not to kiss the ground. A. Lebron is also a proud owner of a nephew and two lovingly supportive parents who all reside on the east coast. You can visit her at www.casualtyofthoughts.tumblr.com and on Instagram @casualtyofthoughts.

Chase M. Ledin received his Bachelor's in English and Sexuality Studies from The Ohio State University and is currently a Master's student in Contemporary Literature, Culture, and Theory at King's College London. His creative writing has been published in *Glitterwolf Magazine*, *A Literation Magazine*, and *Mosaic Magazine*, and he serves as the editor for the Tumblr Writers' Directory. Chase currently lives in London, England.

Born East London but now residing amongst the hedge mumblers of rural Suffolk, **P.A.Levy** has been published in many magazines, from 'A cappella Zoo' to 'Zygote In My Coffee' and stations in-between. He is also a founding member of the Clueless Collective and can be found loitering on page corners and wearing hoodies at www.cluelesscollective.co.uk

Katie Lewington is a writer, reader and firm believer in Karma. She has had her work previously published in various online magazine/journals including *After the pause* and on the *breadcrumbs magazine*, *winamop.com*, and *fuckfiction.net* websites. She also has a collection of poetry published as an eBook on Amazon Kindle titled '*Just: a sign of the times*'. You can contact her on Twitter https://twitter.com/Idontwearahat and read more of her poetry on her blog katielewington.blogspot.co.uk.

Poet **Lilrowboat** has a volume of over 1,900 poems and most of his work can be read at lilrowboat.tumblr.com. Poetry,writing and reading is a huge part of life for Lilrowboat and will continue to be for many years to come.

Vancouver-born **Gavin Kokichi Lytton** has spent the past 5 years in Montreal, and is now graduated from Concordia University with a degree in Creative Writing and Philosophy. Most recently published in Metatron, The Blasted Tree, and L'Ecureuil Mort, he is currently working on his first chapbook.

Jessie Lynn McMains is a writer and zine-maker currently based in southeastern Wisconsin. Her prose and poetry have appeared in The Chapess, The Rain, Party, & Disaster Society, Witchsong, Razorcake, Babel, and Word Riot, amongst other places. Visit her website at recklesschants.net, or find her blog at rustbeltjessie.tumblr.com, where she posts about nostalgia, desire, identity, music, wild girls, and her misspent youth.

Debra McQueen's poems have appeared in *The Legendary, Undertow,* and *NEON,* and she has work forthcoming in *The Lake. WORK Literary Magazine* published one of her many scathing resignation letters. In spite of this, she still has a job teaching special education in Soda City, South Carolina. Don't miss her collection, *Bad Girlfriend,* from Singing Bone Press.

David Antonio Moody currently is a writing instructor at Arizona State University and also serves as production editor for *Cortland Review.* He has edited for *Southeast Review, Juked* and *Saw Palm.* David was the recipient of a 2014 AWP Intro Journals Award, and in 2009 he was awarded a Zbar Poetry Prize. His recent poetry appears in *Spillway,* *Streetlight, Eleven Eleven* and *Artful Dodge.* Born into a small Florida river town, David studied creative writing at Florida State University where he performed in the Jack Haskin's Flying High Circus.

Kelly Neal lives, teaches, and writes in central Texas. He received degrees in literature from the University of Texas, and the Bread Loaf School of English. After 25 years of only sharing his poetry with a small sampling of friends, he recently had poems published by The Axe Factory, A Literation, and Uutpoetry. Kelly is currently working on a project based upon the tarot, "Arcana," with his sister Donna Neal, a digital artist and painter. Poetry has kept him on the edge of stability for more than forty years.

Hal O'Leary, having retired from a life in the theatre at age 84, has turned to writing. Now, at age 89, he has been published in 16 different countries. As a secular Humanist, Hal believes that it is only through the arts that one is afforded an occasional glimpse into the otherwise incomprehensible, and for his contributions to the arts, he is a recent recipient of an Honorary Doctor of Humane Letters degree from West Liberty University, the same institution from which he became a college dropout some 60 years earlier.

Teacher, compere, performer and poet, **Winston Plowes** spends his days fine-tuning background noise and rescuing discarded words. These are re-sculpted over a glass of wine into poetry birds he releases by night to fly to new homes in journals and online destinations worldwide. He lives in a floating home in Hebden Bridge, West Yorkshire UK, where he tries to persuade his black cat, 'Fatty' that it's a good idea for her to do the same.
Find out more about his work at his website here – www.winstonplowes.co.uk

Brian Rowe is working toward his MFA in Creative Writing at the University of Nevada, Reno. His poetry has been published in Strong Verse Magazine, and his short fiction has been published in Dreamspinner Press, Fox Cry Review, Mobius Magazine, and Saturday Night Reader. He recently received UNR's Graduate Student Association Award for Outstanding Creative Writer.

Mallory Rowe has been writing poetry for over ten years, but she is currently passionate about haiku and senryu specifically. After graduating from the University of Alabama at Huntsville with a degree in Art History and English, she continued to write poetry in her spare time. Mallory enjoys being outdoors, and she often uses her observations of nature in her work. She is also an avid reader of philosophy and science, from which she draws much inspiration. Her dream has always been to write full-time, and she feels blessed to be able to live that dream. She self-published her first book, *Looking Inward: 50 Haiku for Reflection and Introspection*, on Amazon as a Kindle edition in January 2015 and has been published in several issues of her universities' literary magazines. She is currently working on her next book of haiku and senryu and raising her daughter with her husband, Stephen, in Huntsville, Alabama.

John Saunders is a founder member of the Hibernian Writers' Group. His collections are *After the Accident* (Lapwing Press, 2010) and *Chance* (New Binary Press, 2013). One of three featured poets in *Measuring, Dedalus New Writers,* 2012, he was shortlisted in the 2012 inaugural Desmond O'Grady Poetry Competition and is a 2014 Pushcart Nominee. John's poems have appeared in journals in Ireland, the UK and America, on many online sites, and been included in *The New Binary Press Anthology of Poetry, The Stony Thursday Book, The Scaldy Detail* 2013, *Conversations with a Christmas Bulb* (Kind of a Hurricane Press, 2013), *The Poetry of Sex,* (Penguin, 2014), *Fatherhood Anthology* (Emma Press UK, 2014), and *The Fate of Berryman Anthology* (Arlen House, 2014).

David Seaman has previously been read in publications like Slice, Bluffs Literary, and Absinthe magazines. He is married to a woman, five dogs, and three exotic birds. David's day job is as a peer recovery specialist for the mentally ill. At times the words for his poetry have been beaten out of him by the symptoms of his own mental struggles. He is an English major and recently interviewed for Poet's Voice Podcast: http://poetsvoices.podbean.com/e/david-seaman-poet-and-fiction-writer/
He can be reached at: dseaman77@gmail.com.

Emily Strauss has an M.A. in English, but is self-taught in poetry, which she has written since college Over 250 of her poems appear in a wide variety of online venues and in anthologies, in the U.S. and abroad. The natural world is generally her framework; she also considers the stories of people and places around her and personal histories. She is a semi-retired teacher living in California.

Brittany Tacconi is a Houston based writer who refuses to plant her garden in the suburbs. Her work has appeared, or is forthcoming, in: *Glass Mountain, Houston & Nomadic Voices, PMS,The Concho River Review, The Griffin,* and *The Oklahoma River Review.* If you can't find her at home with her family try the local bar; she's the one rolling her eyes at the person who requests their rocks with "light ice."

Strident yet curiously engaging, **Laura Taylor** is a poet with a penchant for upsetting apple carts. A regular performer at festivals, gigs and fundraisers, she speaks of love and politics, injustice and hypocrisy, of barking dogs and making space; equality for all.
http://www.writeoutloud.net/profiles/laurataylor
https://www.facebook.com/pages/Laura-Taylor-Poet

Laura Thiessen endeavors to be a vegetarian, but misses seafood and will occasionally cheat. After an extended recess, she has returned to school to obtain a degree in English, but don't ask her if teaching has been her lifelong goal. The answer is a resounding no. In her free time she enjoys video games and margaritas. Although, she certainly doesn't do both at the same time. More of Laura's poetry and other writing can be found on her blog: http://pomegranatepithos.tumblr.com.

Robert Wilson is a writer and poet from Morgantown, WV whose work is often described as dark, beat, and confessional. Aside from writing he enjoys music, video games, reading, coffee, and chocolate. You can email him at Robertjw4688@gmail.com and find him on tumblr at robertjw4688.tumblr.com

Make your own RoguePoetry

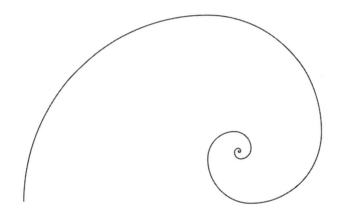

Make your own RoguePoetry instructions:

1. Read the poetry in this book.

2. Feel inspired.

3. Take one step outside of your poetry comfort zone.

4. Now take another.

5. Write!

6. Write a haiku. Write a pantoum. Write a sonnet.

7. Write with spacing abandon. Throw structure to the wind.

8. Write with passion.

9. Write about birds. About socks. About the difference between chocolate syrup and hot fudge.

10. Choose your metaphor and carry it through.

11. Write to be read.

12. Share what you've written. Show it to your best friend. Take a picture and share it online. Tag it #RoguePoetry to share it with us.

13. Or share it privately. Keep it safe. And, when the time comes, submit your new poems to RoguePoetry Review 2016!

Make your own **RoguePoetry**

Make your own **RoguePoetry**

Make your own **RoguePoetry**

Make your own **RoguePoetry**

Make your own **RoguePoetry**

31096636R00064

Made in the USA
Middletown, DE
19 April 2016